WHOLE
PHAT
AND
GLUTEN
FREE
POETRY

WHOLE PHAT AND GLUTEN FREE POETRY

CAROL DURANT

Cover design by The Troy Book Makers
Book design by The Troy Book Makers

Printed in the United States of America

The Troy Book Makers • Troy, New York • thetroybookmakers.com

To order additional copies of this title, contact your favorite local
bookstore or visit www.tbmbooks.com

ISBN: 978-1-61468-397-1

Thanks to my family and friends
for your support and positivity

Shout out to my Godchildren:
Nina, Abby, Jade and Harry

Special thanks to my peeps,
my people & editor

CREATIVE LADIES

What you have in store is

Fear no more,

Your time to shine has appeared today;

No more internal stop and stay.

Wringing hands and dry of mouth;

To drop your vision and massage the doubt

Inner strength is rising forth and bursting past

The negative thoughts

We have each other on the path; ascend like
Sherpa's toward horizon's peak

Your quest is fueled by goals in reach.

With your plan in hand, run the table
and bask at last.

EVICTED

Don't bite that hand that feeds you, that feeds
you and you

The faucet could get turned off and you have
to fend to mend

Bellyaches and no crumbs left out—detached

Shut your mouth and do what you're told, your
thoughts may be bold

But you have no ownership of your space and
deal with the monthly rates

And give your stacks to others to mack;

cause you are a renter and although no shame

I'm on the street in 7 days, without boxes and
a bunch of things

Where to go and what to do. I can't cry, I must
act and do

I'm feeling fetal and feeble and need to
rise and fight

Grab my phone and contact my peeps
that's been in my shoes

Loud cries, positive vibes and plenty of leads
and offers of food

Tomorrow, may yield my new address and my
next new space

Temporary again, but not for long. Mission
focused, not cryptic

So, my being will always be grounded,
permanent and never evicted.

BE WOKE

It's a joke that I just became woke, so that
I can see

The injustice that swirls around me

It's a joke that I just became woke so that
I can feel

The tears that flow down my face because
reality is too real

I didn't imagine another killing with blood
spilling on the road and more disdain and pain

Without justice for our gain

It's a joke that I just became woke so that
I can see

You can grab my soul and beat your pole in
front of me and no one dared to tell or dispel

The look of all the joy that evaporated
from me

It's a joke that I just became woke so that
I can see

I needed me, to anchor my thoughts, toss my
THOTs and get myself clean

To make me focus on the struggle that is
in me

It's a joke that I just became woke, so that
I can see

I need to put the oxygen on me to save us
from the enslaved us

And soldier on, while the war waits for the
rage to catch on.

It's a joke that I just became woke, so that
I can see

You can prove that one, can show a direction
to take or pathway to create

While victory imminent or years away, is a
goal with work and dismay

It's a joke that I just became woke, so that
I can see

I need shades to see through the light; that
sometimes blinds me

From seeing the truth that will keep me free

EMPIRE MOTTO

A man from Albany

gained largesse without scrutiny.

A Capital gain and importance remained

despite a heart full of larceny.

WILLFUL WOMAN

There once was a woman named Nan

who ferried without bucket or man

Met a man on the Pike

and stayed overnight

Woke up and remained polite.

TANGIBLE VOID

I feel the silence of the air around me

Your indentation lays on my soul

I touch your hand or respond to your smile.

You are part of my clouded thoughts and

regardless of how many times

I say I'm fine

I internally despise time and I can't rewind.

We are naked and both should be happy

yet I'm so cold and empty

The covers can't contain the warmth that
does not exist.

ACTION
SOUS CHEF

Be free of your negatives by turning
up the positives

the tone is different and your soul
knows it.

Your ears won't sag and your smile
won't drag

therefore, your recipe for better will
not be bitter.

TWO HOLD

I'm a twin and so I share, room in the womb
and same air

Also, have half a birthday and maybe own
room fraternal,

identical, gender to be named always a
focal point,

but shadows would I like to claim we learned
trust, to argue

and resolve every day and without you, no
instant play

no funny faces, learning to swim, fight and
play and not quit

with more of life's milestones that came up
quick like

dating, driving and graduation days, so
without you, I would

have a single view not double attitude.

Always linked to someone else, so I never
walk by myself is

comforting like cookies and milk

OPTION HERE

Every day I glide down the sidewalk to work.

I listen to the catcalls that are not directed
at me

I wonder why you think it's okay to talk loudly
about her buttocks and ample bosom

How long her hair is and how you would like
to have it

between your sweat-filled meaty palms

Do you know how that makes that woman feel?

Do you know how invisible that makes
me feel?

My wheelchair is like a cloaking device to
them I am smart and pretty,

so why do I crave negative attention?

Cause invisible, just ain't fun

RE-FUSED

I thought of you today and remembered that u
had taken me off your social media

It was not because I was rude or eschewed
your rep or gave up some muse

I have no clue what made you askew

I have tried to figure out what I did. I said
something loud or wrong or smiled too long

I usually have better etiquette, but I took a
wrong turn, I suspect.

I spent days and nights with paranoid sheep,
consternation preventing the sleep

Gone are the days that I adored, that we
laughed and poured all the beer,

both cheap and craft, passed out and woke up
to order 40 wings and knots too.

Not a care to think that work was near and the
fun on hold until the next weekend appeared.

Time has passed and it still irks me, but
I hit a point that did alert me:

What if the issue is not mine?

What I did does not exist.

A choice was made that without a sound;

was placed and delivered without failing
a test

or issuing a warning or beating down

So, I now sleep soundly and go forth renewed.

Later, old acquaintance, finally reviewed.

LOBED OUT

My sun illuminates my journey, hoping for a pathway to victory;

Promising nothing but a destination for this hopeful traveler.

Weary from navigating the pot holes of life delivered by internal thoughts or

Covertly by so called friends or DNA relatives.

I walk steadily without sunblock, naked to the rays, thoughts ablaze.

Which could cause my soul to blister and route to be interrupted by gauze and ointment;

In a prone position with a psychiatric nurse who cares.

PJ PROMENADE

I'm set in my ways and I don't want to
change my pajama pants.

I want to wear them everywhere.

Comfort over fashion and your reaction
is hilarious.

Cause you think I'm nefarious and escaped
from the trailer park,

With a beater tee and flip flops,

Strolling like Mrs. Astor down the
Promenade du Walmart.

ONE ARMED SOUL

Oh, Rensselaer, how do I fear the life you want to have?

The Hard Rock looms and neon lights beckon you to play the hard eight;

Right out of the gate and hold your breath.

Will the dice hold the key to change your life?

Nope. The house comes crashing down, wins your money,

But keeps you inside its walls with stars on stage and other games to play.

A full belly and ads on the telly, I'm told I need to keep playing.

I run around and find a chair and settle in for the arm wrestle with a smiley face on front.

I put in my card and start to pump my fist and have my fun and hopefully, a plentiful run.

I pull forward with a mighty grin and pray that I win.

FAKE SENTIMENT

I'm in love with my plastic Santa, He's from China and they make him better.

For all of us to swipe away; For things that we will pack away.

To never use but recuse; Their purpose from our view.

I love my plastic Santa Cause he lives to reveal my shopping spree.

In shopping for hours to and fro,

And collapse in colored lights aglow.

Amidst the tree; Paper, tape and bows.

I test my nerve to buy some more; And get the bargain evermore.

POOF

We were happy, cozied in the warmth of youth,

Bouncing around the mall, collecting fun
and laughs.

Silently, I found your tasks weren't kicks, But
sticks with remnants of death.

Suddenly, I'm smothering and accusing
you, loving and blaming you, hovering and
mothering you.

Now, I'm a ball of pain, broken up yesterday;
Cause your new love holds the fleeting shroud
of dulling your pain. Your new friends are all
zombies too. Sticks rule!

I cry for the old, you and me, cracking on
those monsters on Glee.

Eating and drinking honestly, not constantly.

And one tomorrow I will cry harder, still

As I stand last in line for a glimpse of you
and casket too.

MY END

Going down the road to ruin, I looked left and
kept movin'

Fearful of what I would see.

I crashed all the mirrors in my view—
and dodged the shards in one hop;

And tried to imagine, how this happened.

The end is too near, the darkness cradles
my fear.

I laid my head in my hands and leaked salt—
my eyes on fire-

Awaiting the fire and hoping the burn

Would sear my soul well done

MINOR RELATIONSHIP

I watched you drive away and in my head the display read, Whew!

It started online as chat stew and morphed into afternoon repast;

Evening repartee and intermittent nightly displays sans clothes.

Eventually, calling every day, texting emailing my life away...

All that emoticons can relay, tears and fears in constant view.

Exhausting my thoughts and stamping on my soul.

Time elapsed and so it had to go, to the recycle bin.

I win!

LEXICON BOND

I dream about writing and then I stop.

I dream about writing then I pause.

I dream about writing then I sigh.

I dream about writing and then I awake and don't write. Is it because it takes passion and solace or malice and tears;

Angst and frustration and assuaged fears

What does it take to filet you soul for others to feast?

And find the destination that you have selected, Full blown cues or discreet molecular views.

But they journey with care and the unknown.

Trusting that you, my captain, will always keep the North Star dear and

Never fear the tip of the iceberg or the teeth of Cerberus.

Commence to click, pen, write.

CLOCKWISE

You touched my ass and had my soul

With a rain of dollars near my pole.

I stopped the wiggle and jiggle to look deep into your eyes;

And found with surprise that I was not just a lustful object,

But a rocket of bold business goals.

I'm saving for a house and a spouse with a blog and a dog.

One kid or twins will do, but I spin because I choose to.

Sitting behind a desk is not for me.

I make it rain, for my final day is closer than you know.

SILENT ECHO

I feel the silence of the air around me.

Your indentation lays on my soul.

I can't touch your hand or respond to your smile. You are

part of my cloud and regardless of how many times

I say that I'm fine.

I internally despise time, that

I can't fast forward nor rewind and see you.

HI, GENE

I met a toothless man today, full of joy and
danced on each line of the sidewalk with glee,

So many people passed, glanced with disgust
and scurried out of his path.

Unaware that his positivity was large and
contagious as the gap of his missing teeth,

as he shimmied away, I wondered where
was my joy?

Was it lost in the fuss of the noise in my head
or the dust bunnies living under my bed

Or in a candy bar?

Maybe I should ask the man with tooth decay,

How can I get some to keep my pain at bay?

COW-SOULED

I'm not as dark as you, but my soul and spirit

Has sparked in you, a love of me that freaks
me out.

Inserts in me the spice I crave and the loyalty
made by both of us.

The trust we have is golden and heaves with

Our passionate stares and sweat drying on
our bed.

It emboldens me to smile sweetly

And weep in my dreams.

ET, TU BOO?!

I don't believe you tried to destroy me, in trying to deploy a spy

To keep me in your line of fire.

In perusing our cell bill, I noticed some unfamiliar numbers.

I thought that you were on the take, but instead you decided

To take drastic action with a trusted now former friend.

You both met up to set me up and your thoughts and lips caressed

Each other and you both did not bother to think of me and our connections

That you both decided to Enola Gay.

I noticed that for 40 days straight, that both he and ye were on the same path

Close or far away. It's a small city, we live in,
so coincidence I so can give;

But no one is that lucky or convenient.

I tested the theory halfway through, by
shopping or calling—one or both of you

And seeing from behind a tree or in the car;
your fear, fallen faces and lack of amour.

Score one or four for me, in discovering
your treachery.

I had to plot the same as you two, to out you
both as Judas times two, but how to make
a splash

Without drowning?

To be continued......

THANKS, BUDDY

I just need you to hide the gun.

It's a good thing that my cartoon bubble is invisible.

MADAM REPOSE

Seventy-eight gentlemen have been in my company in the last two months.

I'm such a lovely lady.

What idea do you have about me?

I give them positive expressions and make them feel joy

And look at themselves differently.

What do you think I do and who do you think I am?

I now know that I carry the weight for myself and others

Accept their guilt and their pain

And hug them tighter until they depart.

SKY PEER

Every day, I miss you and that smile makes
me blissful.

We had a great run and 42 tons of fun.

But you took flight from my sight, so once
a day;

I look and high five you in the sky.

Our first groove was due to you

Your knowledge of moves and beats was not
just YouTube.

Your research was deep.

I trusted your face and lived in your space and
we laughed

And spiced up our attitudes

I was there and watched you sigh for the very
last time.

I went numb and cried.

Today, I ride and glance with side eye and
High five you in the sky.

LUCKY STRIKE

A well-lit awning and a bench,

I sit listening to shifting engines and
swagger chat;

Across the street from where I'm at.

Two gentlemen boasting aloud:

Got paid and hoping to get laid.

Some lucky dame.

FINALLY

I can't be with you and compromise my pride.

I can't think of you and keep dreaming of
our coupling;

Like ducklings moving together side by side.

I can no longer wait for you to sever your
current ties,

And choose to be happy, as we stare into
each other's eyes.

I can't continue to feel nauseous and anxious,

As our relationship fractures from the stress
of the unspoken words;

The lack of touch and the waning vocal joys.

I can decide to ice my eyes and conserve the
fire of my internal flame,

And damn the steam of your gaze and silence the staccato of your voice;

As a daily mantra that stains my day.

I can determine my destiny, by the daily quest by me toward change.

An hourly gauge to extend and regulate my fluctuating emotions;

Has challenged my goals

My path is best directed and answered

By me or Siri.

ELIXIR

Stand in the light of love, not in the shade of
negative evil.

Smile because that beat is moving your lips
toward freedom.

Bend toward those who catch your goodness
with arms wide open.

Dip your toes in the mud that made your
friend cry

and rinse away

Their pain with a bear hug and a hula dance
that makes them laugh.

Remember those who can't hug you back
or are unable to live in the real world.

Enjoy the peace that you provide for
someone who has despair.

They don't realize their life can change, if
they care to pound fear into salt,

And soak their pain toward positive gain.